Faster!

Written by Adam and Charlotte Guillain

RISING STARS

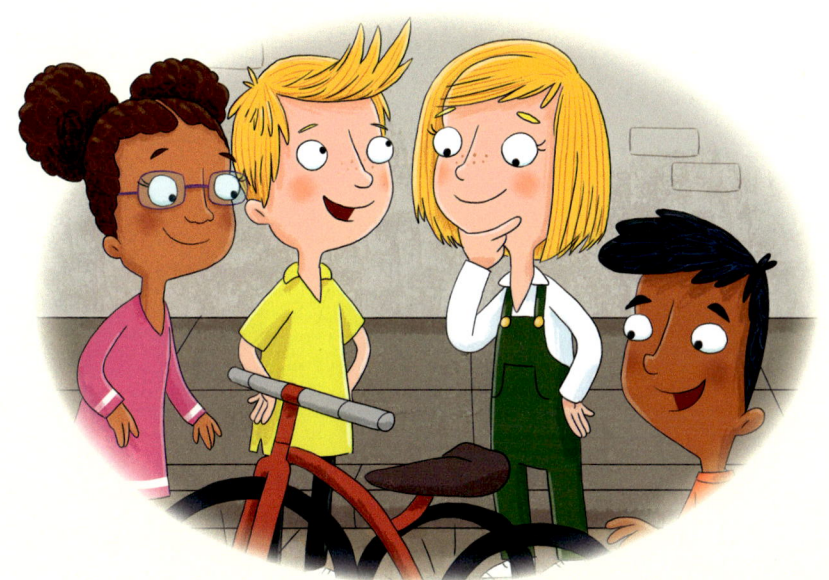

Asha was in a bad mood. She stomped up to her flat and flopped down on the sofa.

"What's up?" asked her dad.

"My bike won't go very fast," moaned Asha. "I need a new one."

Asha's dad went outside with her to see what the problem was.

"Your tyre just needs pumping up," he told her. "But I think everyone's coming in now," he added, looking up at the rain clouds.

Sure enough, all Asha's friends were heading for the flats. Her dad looked at her unhappy face.

"How about I take you all to the museum?" he said. "There's a new exhibition I think you'll like."

Asha's dad left them to look around the exhibition. It was all about bicycles.

As Rav touched one of the old wheels, the lights began to flicker …

The room felt as though it was spinning. They held on to each other and closed their eyes. When they stopped moving, they stared around in amazement.

"I think we've gone back in time!" whispered Asha.

"I wonder where we are," murmured Rav, looking at the cobbled streets.

"Look out!" called Finn, as a tricycle veered round the corner and hurtled towards them.

The boy on the tricycle braked and skidded.

"That was close!" said the boy with a smile. "I was trying to break my record. The trouble is, my tricycle isn't fast enough."

"I have the same problem with my bike," said Asha.

The friends laughed and introduced themselves.

"I'm Johnny," said the boy. "One day, I'm going to be the fastest cyclist in Belfast!"

"We've never been to Belfast before!" said Finn, his eyes wide.

"Can I look at your tricycle?" asked Rav.

Rav felt the hard, rubber tyres. "Is it comfortable?" he asked.

"No," said Johnny. "Riding over these cobbles really hurts my bottom."

"Can I have a go?" asked Tess.

"You can have it for all I care," said Johnny, giving one of the wheels a kick.

They all tried riding the tricycle. The solid, rubber wheels bumped and jolted on the uneven road, making it very painful.

"See? I really need a new one!" Johnny said.

"My bike is slow too," said Asha. "But my dad says it's just the tyres."

Just then, they heard laughter and quick footsteps.

They looked up to find that they were surrounded by lots of children.

"Your clothes are strange," said a little boy.

"Don't be rude to my guests," said Johnny. "They might look different, but they know about cycles."

"Can I have a ride on that?" asked a girl.

"You can have it!" said Johnny again, scowling at his tricycle.

"Really?" said the girl, her mouth open in surprise.

"No, don't," said Asha. "That wouldn't be right."

They looked up to see a man waving at them.

"That's my father," said Johnny. "He's an inventor." He wheeled his tricycle over to the door.

"Cool!" said Asha. "I'd love to talk to him."

"Go ahead," said Johnny. "I'll show your friends around while you're busy."

Johnny led Finn, Tess and Rav to his school. Outside the school gates, children were playing in the street with hoops and marbles while a group of girls played hopscotch.

Meanwhile, Asha wheeled the tricycle into the workshop. Johnny's father waved her inside and called, "Come in! I'll show you the invention I've been working on."

Asha introduced herself.

"I'm John Dunlop," Johnny's father said with a smile.

"Johnny has a problem with his tricycle," said Asha, pointing at a wheel.

"I know," said Mr Dunlop.

Mr Dunlop led Asha to his workbench and showed her a rubber tube.

"Johnny thinks he needs a new tricycle," said Mr Dunlop. "But a tyre filled with air should cushion all the bumps and help the wheels turn much faster."

Asha watched in fascination as the inventor worked.

He soon had two back wheels ready with air-filled tyres.

"Let's go and find Johnny," said Mr Dunlop, his eyes twinkling.

Mr Dunlop and Asha took the tricycle out on to the street just as the others appeared.

"Come and try it now," said Asha.

Johnny frowned, but got on his tricycle slowly. As he pedalled off, his frown turned into a smile.

"It's amazing, Father!" he cried. "I can go so much faster!"

As Johnny disappeared round the corner, the sky turned dark.

"Goodbye, Mr Dunlop!" called Asha, as they felt themselves whirling away.

Back at the museum, Asha looked out of the window, then ran to find her dad.

"It's stopped raining! Let's go home and pump up my tyre," she said. "I want to see how fast I can go!"

Talk about the story

Answer the questions:

1 Why was Asha in a bad mood?
2 What was the name of the boy they met in Belfast?
3 What was the problem with Johnny's tricycle?
4 What does the word 'inventor' mean?
5 Why did the children in Victorian Belfast think the Comet Street Kids' clothes were strange?
6 Why did the new tyres make Johnny's bike go faster?
7 Describe how Johnny's mood changed during the book. How did he feel when the friends first met him? What about at the end?
8 What would you do if your bike had a flat tyre?

Can you retell the story in your own words?